Stuff and Nonsense

Pie Corbett

Chrysalis Education

This US edition copyright © 2006 Chrysalis Education
Published in conjunction with Chrysalis Books Group Plc

International copyright reserved in all countries.
No part of this book may be produced in any form
without written permission from the publisher.

Distributed in the United States by
Smart Apple Media
2140 Howard Drive West
North Mankato, Minnesota 56003

Library of Congress Control Number: 2004108802

ISBN 1-59389-223-3

Associate publisher: Joyce Bentley
Editor and project manager: Nicola Edwards
Designers: Rachel Hamdi, Holly Mann
Illustrators: Andrew Breakspeare,
Sarah Garson, Andrea Huseinovic,
Ley Honor Roberts, Melanie Sharp, Woody

Printed in China

10 9 8 7 6 5 4 3 2 1

Contents

About this book

"Hello. My name is Pie Corbett (yes, I know—silly name, isn't it?). If, like me, you enjoy writing poetry—or even if you think you don't—then this is the book for you! In it, you will find lots of ideas and examples to help you with your writing. You won't need much else—just a pencil, a notebook, and plenty of imagination. Everyone dreams, everyone wonders "what would happen if…" – and that is using your imagination!

Some of the poems in this book are all about looking closely at the world around you and being aware of your senses.

I'll show you how you can use a few poetic techniques to capture forever what you saw and how you felt.

Several of the poems are more about playing with ideas and words. Some have a form to follow—a repeating pattern or a rhyming pattern. For each type of poem, I'll give you an example and then show you step by step how you can write your own version. If you find this hard at first, do not worry—your writing will get better with practice. Just write what you want to write, then reread your poem. Check that you've chosen the best words to help your poem say what you really want it to say."

How to use the book

A poem I've written or one I remember from when I was at school

Poem technique featured

My ideas about the poem

A step-by-step guide to writing your own poem

More ideas for creating similar types of poem

Tips to help you with writing and performing your poems

Use the chart on page 5 to find out about the poems included in the book and the poetic techniques they feature. The chart also lists well-known examples of the same types of poem.

Poem	Type	Features	Other examples
Yesterday	Patterned poem List poem Humorous poem	Adjectives Extending sentences Senses	Poem for my Nephew —Nikki Giovanni
The Rainbow **The Snail** **The Worm**	Shape poems	Making shapes with words	The Tail —Lewis Carroll
The Animal Ark	Tongue twisters	Alliteration Adjectives	Betty Botter —anon.
Freaky Week	Patterned poem Humorous poem Rhyming poem	Days of the week Colors Rhymes	A Monster Alphabet —Gervase Phinn
Doctor Knickerbocker	Playground chant Action rhyme Performance poem	Rhythm	Incy Wincy —anon.
When I Blew the Magic Dust	List poem Patterned poem	Personification Word play	Where Would You Be? —Karla Kuskin
What Am I?	Riddles Word play	Senses	A Moth—from the Exeter Book
Silly Alphabet People	Nonsense poem Rhyming poem Alphabet poem	Rhymes	Mrs. Brown —anon.
Ten Parrots in a Tree	Counting rhyme	Rhymes	Two Little Dicky Birds —anon.
Humpty Dumpty Goes Bananas	Nursery rhyme	Rhymes Language play	Humpty Dumpty —anon.
Marbo the Monster	Performance poem Rhyming poem Humorous poem	Rhymes	The Marog —R. C. Scriven
In the Giant's Rucksack	Nonsense poetry Humorous poem	Invented words	On the Ning Nang Nong —Spike Milligan

Yesterday

Yesterday was a funny day.
I thought I saw all kinds of things:

Yesterday, I saw a gray cat creeping across the park.

Yesterday, I saw a brown dog sitting by the pond.

Yesterday, I saw a black horse trotting in a field.

Yesterday, I saw a red and yellow parrot swooping from the trees.

Yesterday, I saw a pink worm waving to me.
I thought: that's funny!

About this poem

" I enjoyed writing this funny poem because it made me laugh! Can you guess which of the things didn't happen? "

Over to you

Here is how you can make up your own funny poem. You could make your opening lines the same as mine:

> Yesterday, was a funny day.
> I thought I saw all kinds of things:

Now make a list of real things that you did see:

> Yesterday, I saw a car whizz down the road.
> Yesterday, I saw someone running to catch a bus.

Then, to make your poem funny, make the final thing in your list something that it would be impossible for you to see:

> Yesterday, I saw a tree whispering to the grass.

You could make your last line the same as mine:

> I thought: that's funny!

More ideas

Try other openings, like these:
Over the hill you can see...
In my magical world I saw...
I would love to see...

Writing tips

Try adding in some describing words to make your poem more interesting:

Yesterday, I saw a car.
Yesterday, I saw a **shiny** car.

Try adding to the sentence to make something sound impossible:

Yesterday, I saw a shiny car.
Yesterday, I saw a shiny car **flying down the street**.

The Rainbow

The rainbow curves like a bridge of color.

The Snail

My shell curves
Like a rainbow.
I carry my house Upon my back.

The Worm

The worm wriggles like a soft shoelace.

About these poems

❝ I like making shapes with my poems. When you are writing a poem, you can make patterns on pages with words. ❞

Over to you

It is a lot of fun to make shapes with your poems. First, decide what you want to write about, e.g. a snake or the moon, and draw the outline of your subject very faintly.

Now think carefully about the subject you've chosen and write down some words to describe it.

The diamond snake slithers silently through the grass.
The silver moon floats like a coin.

Finally, use your words to create a picture on the page.

The silver moon floats like a coin.

The diamond snake slithers silently through the grass.

More ideas

Try writing shape poems about:

a wizard's hat

the sun

rain falling

a mountain

THE ANIMAL ARK

The lazy lion lay
on the lifesaver.

The tired tiger tasted two
tiny trees.

The kind camel clapped
for the crab.

The happy hippo hid
a hairy hat.

The mischievous monkey
mixed a mud pie.

The jolly giraffe jumped
in the jelly.

About this poem

" I like this poem because the words often start with the same sound. It's fun to hear people read it out loud. Try saying the lines quickly and see how hard it can be! "

Over to you

Try writing a tongue-twisting poem yourself. First, make a list of some animals that you like:

> cat, dog, mouse

Now write a sentence for each animal. Use lots of words that start with the same sound.

> The crafty cat caught a creeping caterpillar.

> The dull dog dug a deep ditch dirtily.

When you have words close to each other that start with the same sound, this is called "alliteration."

More ideas

Here are some other animals you could write about:

ape, buzzard, cow, donkey, emu, fox, giraffe, horse, lion, ostrich, snake, tiger, worm, yak

Try writing tongue twisters about your friends:

Poor Peter put a pot of peanuts on a pretty plate.

Writing tip

If you cannot find words that make sense, have fun and use a nonsensical idea:

The marvelous mouse messed up a mince pie.

Freaky Week

On Monday, I wore white
And had a
terrible
fright.

On Thursday, I wore brown
And turned into
a clown.

On Tuesday, I wore green
And bumped into the queen.

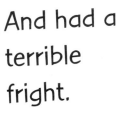

On Friday, I wore pink
And made a
mountain shrink.

On Wednesday,
I wore black
And hid inside
a sack.

On Saturday, I wore red
And lay on a
feather bed.

On Sunday, I wore blue
And kissed a bird or two...

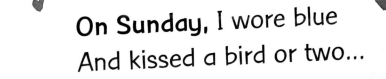

About this poem

" I used the pattern of the days of the week to help me write this poem. I wrote about the different colors that I wear on each day of the week. All kinds of strange things seem to have happened! "

Over to you

Try writing your own rhyming poem about what happens during a week when you wear a different color every day. First, choose a color and write down the opening line:

On Monday, I wore red

Now you have to find a rhyme for the color you have chosen. Then make up the second line:

On Monday, I wore red
And saw a flying bed.

Your ideas don't have to make sense. In fact, the more nonsensical your ideas, the funnier your poem will sound!

More ideas

Try writing a poem using the months of the year. In each month, you might see a different animal, e.g.:

In January, I saw a cat
Climbing up a clown's hat.

Writing tips

Make a list of rhyming words for each color to help you choose a rhyme, e.g.:

Green—bean, jelly bean, machine, queen, sardine, windscreen...

White—dynamite, flight, headlight, kite, knight, midnight, night...

Black—back, crack, pack, quack, sack, shack...

If you get stuck for a rhyme, use a rhyming dictionary or the alphabet to help. See how I have used the alphabet to find rhymes for "red":

bed   fed   head   led

a b c d e f g h i j k l m
n o p q r s t u v w x y z

said, shed   ted   wed

Doctor Knickerbocker

Doctor Knickerbocker, Knickerbocker
Number TEN!
Hold up hands and show ten fingers.

Now we've got the rhythm of the street,
Let's get the rhythm of the hands.
Clap hands twice—clap clap.

Now we've got the rhythm of the hands,
Let's get the rhythm of the feet.
Stamp feet twice—stamp stamp.

Now we've got the rhythm of the feet,
Let's get the rhythm of the knees.
Slap knees twice—slap slap.

Now we've got the rhythm of the knees,
Let's get the rhythm of the hips.
Wiggle hips twice—wooo weee.

Now we've got the rhythm of the hips,
Put it all together and what have you got?

Clap clap, Stamp stamp, Slap slap, Wooo weee!

Clap hands twice, stamp feet twice, slap knees twice, wiggle hips twice.

About this poem

" This playground rhyme sounds really good if a group of people chant it together. Try chanting it with your friends in a sing-song voice. Do the actions, too! "

Over to you

You could make up some more lines for Doctor Knickerbocker, following the same pattern. First, think of a part of your body that you could use to make an action, e.g. teeth biting or finger clicking.

Next, put your ideas into the pattern:

> Now we've got the rhythm of the hips,
> Let's get the rhythm of the teeth.

> Now we've got the rhythm of the teeth,
> Let's get the rhythm of the fingers.

Don't forget to tell people how to do the actions:

> Bite teeth together to make a sound twice—bite bite.
> Click fingers together to make a sound twice—click click.

Performance tips

Stand together in a group, with one person standing slightly in front. Follow this person's lead so that you all keep in time. When you are performing the poem, think:

- Can the words be heard clearly?
- Are you all saying each line at the same time?
- Does the poem sound lively and fun?

 Writing tip

Here are some ideas for other actions you could include:

- Eyes—close/open
- Head—nod nod
- Nose—parp parp
- Cheeks—puff puff

When I Blew the Magic Dust

When I blew the magic dust—
The trees shivered in the woods
And the rivers trembled.

When I blew the magic dust—
The mountains hid their heads
And the streets pulled on their coats.

When I blew the magic dust—
The clocks grinned at the carpets
And the chairs tiptoed out of the room.

When I blew the magic dust—
The teacher turned to stone
And the children became statues.

About this poem

" One day I was wondering what might happen if I could blow magic dust into the world. I wrote this list poem and imagined how the dust might bring things alive. "

Over to you

Imagine that you are in a movie and someone gives you a handful of magic dust. The dust can bring anything alive. You can make anything happen. You can make cars fly and mountains speak!

Before you start writing, make a list of the things that you want to sprinkle the dust upon. They could be objects you see at home:

> table, chair, cup, saucer, pencil, ruler, knife, fork, wall, cell phone

Or they could be things you notice outside:

> houses, flowers, trees, moon, stars, clouds, sun

Now write some lines to say what happens:

> When I blew the magic dust—
> The cups marched into the cupboard
> And the mobile phone ran away.
>
> When I blew the magic dust—
> The houses sneezed and begin to sing.
>
> When I blew the magic dust—
> The trees got off their knees and
> went for a walk.

More ideas

Instead of throwing "magic dust," you could begin each line of your poem with a different opening:

When I waved my wand—
When I clapped my hands—
When I clicked my fingers—

WHAT AM I?

What am I?

I race down your street,
But you cannot see me.

I make trees bend down
And the grass shiver.

I help kites fly high
And wrinkle the waves.

What am I?

I am round as a ball,
But you can never kick me.

You can feel me most days
But will never touch me at all.

I keep you warm.

What am I?

I am awake when you slee

I am as silver as a coin,
But you will never spend m

I look like an eye
But cannot see.

About this poem

" Riddles are like jokes. You have to hide the truth. Did you guess the answers to these riddles? They were about the wind, the sun, and the moon. "

Over to you

Writing riddles is lots of fun. Make up some of your own and see if your friends can guess the answers.

First, you have to think of a subject for your riddle, e.g. *the sun*.

Now you have to give the reader clues without giving away what you are writing about. To help you do this, think about what your subject looks like:

I am like a plate,
But you will never eat off of me.

Next, think about any sounds it makes:

I am as silent
As a stone.

Finally, think about what it does:

I am hotter than chili,
But you will never taste me.

More ideas

Here are some other subjects for riddles:

mist, stars, night, a clock, a key, a lock, a pond, a stream, a frog, a raindrop, a rainbow, a hand, a shoe

Writing tip

Try thinking about what other people think of your subject. Include these reactions in your riddle, e.g.

Some people love me,
But others run to hide from my glare.

Silly Alphabet People

Mrs. A
Ate some hay.

Mrs. B
Climbed a tree.

Mrs. C
Scratched her knee.

Mrs. D
Lost her key.

Mrs. E
Saw a chimpanzee.

Mrs. F
Called for Jeff.

About this poem

" Here is a rhyming poem that is based on the alphabet. I got the idea when I was wondering how the letters of the alphabet might behave, if each letter was a person. "

Over to you

Choose some letters and use them to write your own alphabet poem.

First, make a list of the letters of the alphabet and try to find some rhymes for each letter, e.g.

I—fly, pie   V—recipe, me
J—tray, day   W—trouble you!

You don't have to include every letter—some are tricky to find a rhyme for (the hardest ones are H, W, and X!).

Pick a letter and write your first line:

Mrs. I

To write the second line, choose a rhyme and make up a short line:

Mrs. I
Ate a fly.

Do this for as many letters as you choose, until your poem is complete.

More ideas

You could write a poem using numbers instead of letters:

Mr. One
Had lots of fun.
Mr. Two
Saw a kangaroo.
Mr. Three
Hurt his knee....

Ten Parrots in a Tree

I saw ten parrots in a tree.

One for a sneeze,
two for a chick,

three for surprise,
four for a brick.

Five for a friend,
six for a chair,

seven for a letter,
eight for a bear.

Nine for a crow,
and ten for snow,

those are the parrots
that sat in a row.

About this poem

" In this poem, I made up a new counting rhyme for parrots—my favorite bird! There are counting rhymes for all kinds of things, from cherry pits on a plate to magpies perching on the branch of a tree. "

Over to you

You could make up a counting rhyme for boats on the sea or clouds in the sky—or anything you like! Let's say you wanted to make up a counting rhyme about cars.
First, write the opening line:

I saw ten cars whizzing by.

Next, list the numbers:

One for a ....   two for a ...

Now add either an animal or an object to complete the first line:

One for a mouse

Then think of a rhyme and complete the second line:

One for a mouse, two for a house.

You could try to make the lines for numbers three and four, five and six, seven and eight, and nine and ten rhyme with each other:

Three for a cake, four for a snake.

You could end your poem with the line

Those are the cars that went whizzing by.

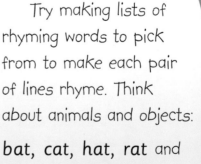

Writing tip

Try making lists of rhyming words to pick from to make each pair of lines rhyme. Think about animals and objects:

bat, cat, hat, rat and dog, fog, frog, log.

Humpty Dumpty Goes Bananas

Humpty Dumpty sat on the wall,
Eating green bananas.
Where do you think he put the skins?
Down the King's pajamas!

Humpty Dumpty sat on a wall,
Eating an apricot.
Where do you think he put the pit?
—In the Queen's best teapot!

Humpty Dumpty sat on a wall,
Eating some whipped ice cream.
What do you think happened next?
Humpty had a bad dream!

Humpty Dumpty sat on a wall,
Eating an apple pie.
What do you think he did with the crust?
Threw it into the sky!

About this poem

66 When I was in school, we used to change lots of well-known rhymes to make them funny. This is one of my favorite nursery rhymes. I've had lots of fun playing around with it. 99

Over to you

You can write your own version of Humpty Dumpty.

Make your opening line the same:

Humpty Dumpty sat on a wall,

Change the next line so that Humpty is eating something:

Eating scrambled eggs.

Turn the third line into a question, using "what," "where" or "how":

Where do you think he put the shell?

Finally, make the last line rhyme with the second:

Underneath his legs!

Remember—it doesn't matter if your poem doesn't make sense. Just have fun making up rhymes.

More ideas

Try changing other well-known rhymes. At first, keep the changes simple, e.g.

Little Miss Muffet
Sat on a tuffet
Eating her apples and pears.
Along came a spider
That sat down beside her
And frightened Miss Muffet upstairs!

Other rhymes that you can change are:
Simple Simon, Jack, and Jill and Sing a Song of Sixpence.

Marbo the Monster

Marbo the Monster eats any old stuff.
He eats and he eats, till he's had just enough.

He eats trees and bushes,
Bulldozers and bones,
Telephones and turnips,
Skyscrapers and stones.

He eats swings and ponds,
Dinosaurs and doors,
Ice creams and nice cakes,
Flamingoes and floors.

He eats earwigs and candles,
Caterpillars and clouds,
Macaroons and mud,
Castaways and crowds.

Yes, Marbo the Monster
is terribly tough.
He eats and he eats,
till his tummy is
stuffed!

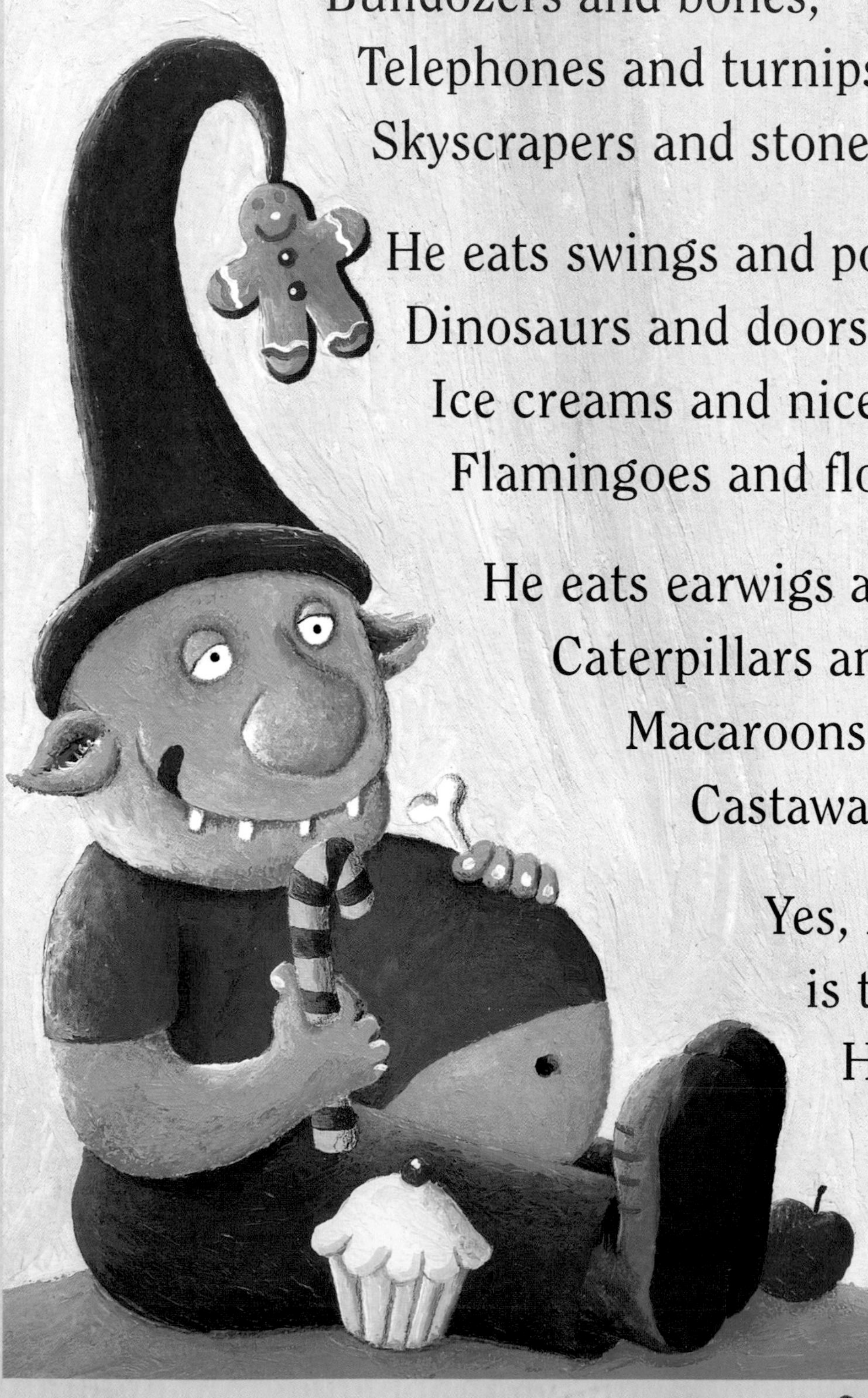

About this poem

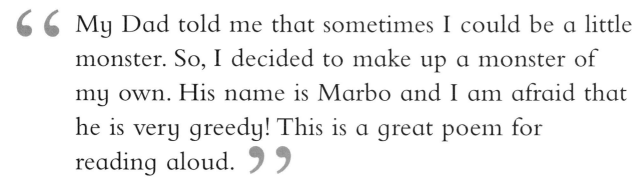

" My Dad told me that sometimes I could be a little monster. So, I decided to make up a monster of my own. His name is Marbo and I am afraid that he is very greedy! This is a great poem for reading aloud. "

Over to you

You could make up your own monster poem to perform with your friends.

First, decide on a good name for your monster. You could use my pattern at the start of the poem, but put in your monster's name:

> Munchy the Monster eats any old stuff.
> He eats and he eats, till he's had just enough.

Begin each verse in the same way:

> He eats...

Then say what he eats:

> He eats wheels and taxis,

Next add a second line of two things joined by "and":

> Coffee pots and cheese,

Now add a third line:

> Basketballs and bookshops,

The last line has to rhyme with the second line (cheese):

> Haircuts and honeybees.

 **Performing tips**

Try reading the poem aloud in a rhythmic and sing-song way. It works well if you learn the rhyme with a group.

You could add some simple percussion for a background beat.

Your voices could become louder as you speak each verse, ending with an explosion as you shout the last line!

In the Giant's Rucksack

In my rucksack I keep—
A squidgy to wash behind my ears
Like my mommy told me.

In my rucksack I keep—
A grabbler to frighten off lions
And princesses to be rescued.

In my rucksack I keep—
A warmkin to wrap around me
When the wind is cold
And my nose turns red as a robin's chest.

In my rucksack I keep —
A crunge to blip my friends with
When we meet each other
Or they don't see me coming.

In my rucksack I keep —
A tingle to play when I am singing
Myself to sleep at night.

About this poem

" If giants did exist they might have their
own language. So I made up some things
that a giant might keep in a rucksack. "

Over to you

The exciting thing about writing a poem like this
is that you can make anything up.

First, write down the same opening line:

> In my rucksack I keep—

Then invent a word

> In my rucksack I keep—
> A squirtle...

Now say what it does or what it is for:

> In my rucksack I keep—
> A squirtle to catch my tears...

Finally, add more to the verse,
if you can.

> In my rucksack I keep—
> A squirtle to catch my tears
> When I see something sad.

Writing tip

As well as inventing words such
as "squirtle" and "crunge," you can mix
up words to make new words, like this:

First, list some words:

counting	newspaper
toolkit	backward

Next, split the words in half:

count/ing	news/paper
tool/kit	back/ward

Now move the parts around to make
a set of new words:

countpaper	newsing
toolward	backkit

A Poet's Toolbox
Creating patterns and special effects

 ## How to write your poem

You can write a poem
like a list with a repeating line:

I wish I could fly in the sky.
I wish I could pick up a cloud.
I wish I could play catch with the stars.

You can make your poem
into a shape on the page:

Eye spy with
my
little eye

You can use a rhyme at
the ends of lines:

I thought I saw a dinosaur
Flying in the air.
You never saw a dinosaur.
Yes—I saw it over there!

Two things that you can do in a poem

1. You can try to say what
something is really like:

I saw a slim cat
Slip along the back wall
With eyes like diamonds.

2. You can play with ideas and
create something nonsensical:

I saw a red bus grow wings
and start to sing.

How to use special effects

Here are some of my favorite special
effects that we have looked at in this book:

Choose good words:

The **growling** tiger **prowled**
under the **tall** trees

builds a stronger picture than

The **big** tiger **went**
under the **trees**.

Think of unusual ideas:

I dreamed I saw a chair
that could dance.

Try some alliteration:

The **dirty dog dug** a **deep ditch**.

How to polish your poems

When you have finished writing a poem, reread
it and look for places where you could improve it.

Add some descriptive words:

I saw a bear in the woods.
I saw an **old** bear in the **dark** woods.

Say more to build a clearer
picture in your readers' minds:

I saw an old bear in the dark woods
Standing by the dashing river.

Use alliteration:

I saw a **big bear**
By the **bridge**.

Now show your poem to someone else
to see what they think of it.

31

Glossary

alliteration A few words that begin with the same sound, e.g. two tiny tigers told a turtle to tickle its toes.

anon. A shortened word that stands for "anonymous," which means no one knows who wrote the poem!

counting rhyme A rhyme that is based on counting.

playground rhyme A well-known rhyme that is chanted by school children.

rhyme A rhyme happens when words share the same end sound pattern, e.g. cog, dog, fog, log.

riddle A puzzle where the subject has to be guessed.

shape poem A poem written in the shape of the subject.

tongue twister A short line or poem that uses alliteration and is difficult to say.

Index